I0211815

# Crossings 35

# The Story of a Jewish Boy

All rights reserved. Parts of this book may be reprinted only by written permission from the authors, and may not be reproduced for publication in book, magazine, or electronic media of any kind, except in quotations for purposes of literary reviews by critics.

© 2022, Leopold Berman
© 2022, Translation by Giuliana Carugati
© 2022, Introduction by Simi Berman
© 2022, Afterword by Simi Berman and Nicholas Grosso
Cover image by Simi Berman

Library of Congress Cataloging-in-Publication Data

Names: Berman, Leo, 1931-2003, author. | Carugati, Giuliana, translator.
Title: The story of a Jewish boy / by Leopold Berman ; translated by Giuliana
   Carugati.
Other titles: Storia d'un ragazzo Ebreo. English
Description: New York, NY : Bordighera Press, [2022] | Series: Crossings ; 35 |
   Summary: "'This is the face of a boy whose youth was taken from him, who
   doesn't know anymore how to cry or laugh, that life has crushed under the
   inhuman weight of cruel reality. In this photograph you see the mask of a face;
   if that mask were lifted you would see a mind troubled by life that too cruelly
   torments your son,' Leopold Berman wrote his father in a postcard sent shortly
   after leaving a refugee camp. 'The Story of a Jewish Boy' recounts the horrors
   and fleeting hopes of a boy and his family trying to survive the final days of
   World War II in Italy"-- Provided by publisher.
Identifiers: LCCN 2022019399 | ISBN 9781599541921 (trade paperback)
Subjects: LCSH: Berman, Leo, 1931-2003--Diaries. | Cinecittà (Displaced
   persons camp) | Jews--Italy--Biography. | Jewish children in the Holocaust--
   Italy--Biography. | Holocaust, Jewish (1939-1945)--Italy--Personal narratives.
   | World War, 1939-1945--Refugees--Italy.
Classification: LCC DS135.I9 B47 2022 | DDC 940.53/180830945--dc23/
   eng/20220511
LC record available at https://lccn.loc.gov/2022019399

Printed by Ingram Lightning Source.

Published by
BORDIGHERA PRESS
John D. Calandra Italian American Institute
25 W. 43rd Street, 17th Floor
New York, NY 10036

Crossings 35
ISBN 978-1-59954-192-1

# the story of a jewish boy

BY LEOPOLD BERMAN

Translated by Giuliana Carugati

BORDIGHERA PRESS

# TABLE OF CONTENTS

# INTRODUCTION
by Simi Berman

This is the diary and writings of Leopold (Leo) Berman(n), a teenage boy living through the last days of World War II and the early post-war years in Italy.

His mother, Anna Tuch, was a strikingly beautiful young woman from Lvov, Poland. She came to Merano with her mother, after the death of her father, to be treated at Waldpark, the sanitorium Leo's grandfather, Maximillian Bermann, had opened, which had become famous for its grape cure, where patients would eat half a pound of the blue hard-skinned grapes from the surrounding vineyards three times a day for four to six weeks between September and October.

At Waldpark, Anna met Siegfried (Friedl) Bermann, Dr. Bermann's sophisticated and debonair son, who had studied soil agronomy at the University of Perugia with the intention of becoming a pioneer in Palestine. Anna and Friedl fell in love and became engaged. Soon after, Friedl wanted Anna to go with him to Palestine, but with Anna unprepared to follow after him, he went alone. When he returned a year later, they were married, though his interest in her had cooled while he was away.

After the marriage, Friedl and Anna lived at Waldpark along with Friedl's parents, brothers, and sister. In 1929, Leo's brother Raffaele was born, and Leo in 1931. Their first six years were spent in the cushioned environment of their grandfather's sanitorium, The garden, however, was Leo's own private Eden, luxuriant and secure. He climbed its fig trees, plucked its apples, and lost himself among the roses, tall grasses, and other vegetation. He was a playful and athletic boy who loved to run and ride his bicycle up and down the hills around the sanitorium.

Raffaele (Ralfi) on the other hand, at the age of four, was placed in a clinic in Rapallo, on the Italian Riviera, to be treated for an inflammation of the lining of the lungs, never fully recovering his health and strength. One illness led to another; typhus, then tuberculosis of the bone, following him for the rest of his life.

In 1935, Friedl Bermann took the family from Merano to Milan where he opened a chemical factory to manufacture detergent. At this time, things had already begun to deteriorate, both in the marriage and with respect to the situation of the Jews in Italy.

During the next seven years, Mussolini's policy turned more aggressively racist as his alliance with Hitler strengthened. The edict of 1938, among other restrictions, forbade Jews from attending schools and Jewish teachers from teaching in them. Leo had had one year of school, from the ages of six to seven in Milan before the edict was enacted

In 1939, with a sense of impending disaster and a growing distancing of himself from his wife and sons, Friedl Bermann sailed to America. His delay in sending tickets for his family resulted in Anna, Rafaele, and Leo standing at the port while their ship, The Rex, set sail.

Stranded in wartorn Italy, Anna decided to go back to Merano with the boys. Though by now Merano was not safe for Jews, it was a place she knew and had personal resources. Nevertheless, they were able to remain there in relative safety until September 8, 1943. On that day, as described by Leo in his account, everything changed dramatically. When the Badoglio government, an interim government that had come to power after the fall of Mussolini, called for an armistice with the Allies, the hopes of all who had suffered during the fascist regime were raised.

In August 1944, after the German retreat from Perugia, Anna, Leo, and Ralfi managed to get a ride to Rome with a British soldier in the back of a jeep. When they arrived in the city, Ralfi was placed in a hospital while Leo and his mother, now homeless, went to live in a Displaced Persons camp at Cinecittà, the film studio in Rome that had been turned into a temporary shelter for refugees.

The Bermanns met many other refugees there, among them Jews from all over Europe, who had survived and found their way to the DP camp in Rome. Stories were exchanged of the terrible ordeals that people had undergone during the course of the war. Leo kept a diary, a day by day account of some of these stories as well as other daily occurrences that were significant to him. He also took this opportunity, at age 14, to write *Story of a Jewish Boy*, an account of his experiences of the previous one and a half years.

# diary

*of*

# leopold
# berman

## APRIL 12, 1945
## ROME

Uncle Hennek is leaving at 3 o'clock to go to an U.N.R.R.A.[1] rest home. This home is located on the via Cassia.

Ralfi has been sick for several days, but yesterday he had a very high fever. Mamma is very worried about him. Also Aunt Ada is not feeling well and has a small cough. The trial of Nazi criminals is taking place in Nuremberg. The American prosecutor yesterday has read an extremely secret document with regard to Czechoslovakia.

The document shows that the gas to subdue Czechoslovakia had been ready.

---

1 United Nations Relief and Rehabilitation Administration

## MAY 24. 1945
## CINECITTÀ

Yesterday was a day of ugly memories. In the afternoon, photographs of the concentration camps of Buchenwald, Weimar and Dachau were put up in the "bar." I shuddered to think that among those bones could be those of my relatives. At night they showed an even more horrible documentary. One could see living skeletons, mountains of bones, and other scenes impossible to describe. I was speechless during the entire show, thinking how a few men could kill millions of people in cold blood and without distinction. Nothing could be enough punishment for these people. But the thing that made me most angry was that some of these lesser murderers are even here in this camp.

There was significant evidence against these evil-doers. After some Hungarian women spoke against the Jews, the kitchen staff refused to prepare meals for one or two days if these Nazis did not leave the camp.

## MAY 28, 1945
## CINECITTÀ

Yesterday morning we went to the lake at Albano. It is a wonderful place and we had a great time. Coming back, we were lucky to get a ride with a truck from the camp.

I had to stay up until midnight to study, and today I am really tired.

## JUNE 4, 1945
## CINECITTÀ

Two minutes ago I noticed Miriam Theriacovschi, crying outside. My mother told me that she was crying because she had learnt that her mother had been killed by the despicable Nazis.

I thought how fortunate I am still to have my mother. I also thought how many other children are crying for their mothers, and how many mothers for their children. How mournful this crying is, which can be heard even in this room.

## JUNE 5, 1945
## CINECITTÀ

Yesterday five Greek girls arrived from Rhodes who in 1944 had been brought to the camp in Dachau, Germany. They live in the room next to ours. The entire camp talks about them. The things they say are horrible. I will write them down as I heard them. These women have told of how they underwent a daily two-hour session of blows with a stick. Worst of all is that they told of having had to see their parents burn.

Everyone felt great pity for those girls who were helped in many ways here in the camp. They were given clothes and some beds. Every day one hears about more Nazi atrocities. Let us not forget them.

## JUNE 6, 1945
## CINECITTÀ

Tonight when I came back home, I found one of those Jewish women from Greece in our room. This girl had been taken by the SS from Rhodes to Auschwitz. There her parents and sisters were burnt. She was made to work because she wasn't either sick or too thin. The fact is that someone who only had a tiny blemish wasn't taken for work. From Auschwitz they were taken to Dachau in Germany. There she was made to unload pitcoal from train wagons and to cover craters made by bombs. On her arm she had a number branded by the SS.

## JUNE 9, 1945
## CINECITTÀ

Today mother is very nervous because we don't have any money and because of Ralfi. Every trifle gets her mad. I try to control myself as best I can, but sometimes nasty words escape me; afterwards I regret it bitterly. I really feel sorry for dear mother. All alone as she is, having to take care of me and Ralfi is certainly not an easy thing.

Here in Rome it is unbearably hot, and even the Egyptians say it is not as hot in their country.

I have a lot of work to do, because on the 25th I must take my exams.

## JUNE 12, 1945
## ROME

Today I went to visit Ralfi. He looks run down to me. The doctor says that he has influenza. After lunch, he had a fever of 38 degrees (centigrade).

## JUNE 13, 1945
## CINECITTÀ

Mother has decided to leave Cinecittà. We are going to Rome to the Pingis. In our room everything is upside down. So this sojourn has ended as well. We arrived in Cinecittà on August 29, 1944. Ten long months. Many things have happened. The war has ended, as well as many other things. My handwriting is not very natural because I am very excited.

## JUNE 13, 1945
## ROME

We are by now in Rome. We got here about half an hour ago. It's very nice here. There is a bedroom and a dining room; the furniture is brand new. The kitchen is very small but it doesn't matter. One thing that pleases me very much is the bathroom, because at Cinecittà it was really disgusting. I do not regret leaving the camp because it is more comfortable here.

I realize now that today is the 13th. Some people say it's badluck, but it seems the opposite to me.

## JUNE 19, 1945
## CINECITTÀ

It's Sunday today, and since I have finished almost all of my homework, I am very bored. So as not to sit doing nothing, I will write of something that happened during our flight. We were at Brogio, a village of four or five houses near Perugia. It was the 16th or 17th of June 1944, I don't remember very well.

At about 10 o'clock in the morning we saw a good number of German vehicles arrive, fleeing from the battle front, which was at that time near.

First came two tanks provided with anti-aircraft guns, which however were damaged. Afterwards came several cars and trucks. One of these, and precisely the one which was used as a machine-shop and had a generator in tow, stopped right in front of our house. That very morning the Allied airforce attacked the vehicles and we had a terrible fight because the Spitfire bullets were hailing down all around us. One thing was reassuring to us, another scared us.

## JUNE 21, 1945
## ROME

The exams are four days away. I must try to pass with an 8 average, otherwise I won't be able to take the "terza media" (eighth grade) exams in September. Dear mother promised that if l do well she'll buy me a stamp album for my stamps. We like it in our new house. In the past few days I have been a little sick to my stomach. When I sit down for a meal I think how nice it would be to eat once with dear father and Ralfino. A really nice foursome. Last night I went for a walk with mother in the streets of Rome. Near here is the club for Jewish soldiers, and from the window the Jewish flag hangs. How beautiful to finally see our flag wave free among all the others.

## JULY 4, 1945
## ROME

Today I finally took my exams. What a relief. This morning there were the oral exams and it went well. I achieved an 8 average. This afternoon mother gave me 250 lire as a present for the exam. I bought myself an automatic pencil. These days the electoral campaign is going on in England. Churchill gives several speeches every day. Tomorrow is election day in England.

In Italy as well they have just changed government. Ferrucio Parri has been designated as Prime Minister. In Rome one can see signs of all kinds, such as W IL COMMUNISMO, and W LA DEMOCRAZIA CRISTIANA, and a lot more nonsense. I have noticed that now there are many Brazilians in the city. Ralfi is not cured yet. In my opinion the doctor is a loafer who is simply trying to pocket as much money as possible. Last month he was saying that Ralfi would be well by mid-July, but now he has changed his mind and says that he doesn't know how long the disease will continue.

In Rome the price of goods has gone down considerably, given that a lot is pouring in from Northern Italy.

## JULY 9, 1945
## ROME

On July 4th I took my exams, which were a huge success. Here are the grades which I learnt yesterday from my teacher: Latin 8, History and Geography 8, Art 8, Math 10. These grades have passed my expectations by a lot. I was particularly happy about math, because getting 10 in junior high school is a very rare event. In about twenty days I will resume studying in order to be able to enter "terza media."

Last night when we came back home, mother and I had a pleasant surprise. Uncle Kuba, mother's brother, had arrived. We had dinner together and this morning he came to have breakfast at our place. He is at present in Austria with the Jewish Brigade.

## JULY 15, 1945
## ROME

This which I am now writing, if it comes out one day, will be a warning for those who do not want to believe. This is the simple story of one of the many who had been in the concentration camps for five years, tortured by those ferocious beasts, the SS. Calling those monsters ferocious beasts is not enough. Today at the Polish restaurant we met a 19-year-old Polish youth. He did not have a place to stay, and mother took him to our house. The things he told us are almost impossible to retell. If a writer wanted to represent a picture of monstrous facts, he certainly would not be able to write something more horrible. This youth has been left alone in the world, and has had to see with his own eyes his father, mother, sisters and brothers burn. He told us how he saw babies thrown from the third floor, or smashed forcefully against the wall. The most terrible thing he has told is that they castrated eighteen or nineteen-year-old youths. The women were forced to give as much as a liter of their blood to be given to the wounded German soldiers. Life had become so unbearable that one day this youth unbuttoned his shirt and begged an SS to kill him but the soldier answered: "You are still fit for work." If everything were to be told, it would be necessary to write a book, and I hope that such a book will be written. In this way, all this will be brought to light.

These monstrous murderers must all die. Should there be another war against Germany, I will be the first one to volunteer, and I won't feel pity for anyone, just as they have done.

After all I have seen and heard, my hatred for this damned people will never cease.

## JULY 29, 1945
## ROME

A few days ago I started studying again. The exams will be in mid-September. Ralfi has been getting up, and I pray to God to make him recover.

We haven't had any mail from father for a few weeks. His latest letter was sent on June 20th.

Mother has an extremely difficult time bringing food to Ralfi. One must go visit twice a day to bring him lunch and dinner.

Now in England in place of Churchill there is Attlee. Let's hope that they will give us Palestine.

## AUGUST 1, 1945
## ROME

Last night mother was very sick; she was vomiting and I was able to go to bed only at two in the morning. It's terribly hot.

I have started to write the book "STORY OF A JEWISH BOY."

## AUGUST 25, 1945
## ROME

On Friday we went to the beach at Nettuno. It is an enchanting place, but how long did it take before we could get an ambulance. We must thank our dear mother because we are now at the beach. By now I have done a lot of swimming, and also rowing, which is good exercise. Today I came back to Rome because I must study a lot, but I believe that in a few days I will go back to the beach. In the meantime, Ralfi is still there.

The rooms we are renting are quite expensive. Room and board is 550 lire a day per person, which means 49,500 lire a month. Ralfi sunbathes on a large terrace.

The war in Japan is over, but a civil war broke out in China. When will people in the world not fight each other?

# OCTOBER 4, 1945
# ROME

I am ill with malaria, but I hope that in a few days I will be cured, thanks to quinine. Ralfi is still at Nettuno, thank God he is in good health. Mother is with me here in Rome.

Until yesterday I was staying at my teacher's because I had to take my exams during this time and at home I could not study well. The family is very kind to me and I will try to reward them in the future.

We have not had any news from father since August 15th. In his latest letter he writes that he has become an American citizen, and that he will try to have us go to America as soon as possible. Today mother has received two letters from her sister and her Polish brother; they are now staying near Graz in Austria. She also learned that two of her sisters and a brother, together with their children, were killed by the Germans.

This piece of news has saddened mother very much today; she cries continuously, although she tries to hide it from me.

# DECEMBER 9, 1945
## ROME

With the following decree it is clear that we have to leave our apartment within 6 days, namely before the 11th of this month.

But tomorrow mother will ask her lawyer to contest this. If this fails we hope that some employee, who has been paid by us, will enable us to stay in this apartment indefinitely.

It seems to me that Signora Pingi is too interested in this apartment. My opinion is that she is in cahoots with Signor Carozza to send us away by any means possible so that they can sell the furniture which they can't do while we are here. I think Signor Carozza promised a good sum to send us away. Anyway, Signora Pingi is a very shrewd person. We will see.

(Today a letter arrived from Mr. Safier.) I suggested that mother come to some agreement with father, maybe in the following way: Send the separation contract to someone of mutual trust in America. When we arrive in America this person can give this to father.

The day before yesterday Signor Carozza came. We see that Signora Pingi also lies. She had told us that she didn't have a third key to the apartment but now it appears that Signor Carozza has a third key.

## DECEMBER 11, 1945
## ROME

Ralfi is not well. Dr. Marroni drained the pus even from the front where he had pustules before. He also had jaundice. (I believe this has been caused by the upsets that father caused him lately.) Mother is very worried and I don't know how to console her. Tonight I sat at the table and looked at her for a long time. It seems that she has aged at least 10 years in these last weeks. In his last telegram father said he couldn't bring us to America without first having the separation papers. Mother would give them to him if it was sure that father would bring us to America. But this is not very probable. I will explain in more detail.

## DECEMBER 15, 1945
## ROME

Today I had to admit a bitter fact, that it is much better to be nasty than to do good. If one is nasty, one is respected by everyone, while a good person is stepped on.

The more I think of father, the more I find him despicable. It would be difficult for me to respect him during my lifetime. What he has done has been too base and dirty.

Yesterday, the Officer of Finance (Guardia di Finanza) came to requisition the apartment and the lock will be taken down tomorrow.

## DECEMBER 22, 1945
## ROME

I was at the cinema a little while ago. A man followed me as soon as I left the house. This is the second time it happened. I would like to know who sends these gentlemen. (I didn't know I had beautiful hair but today that gentleman told me that when I left the house.) I was quite amused to lead him around town a little. When I turned around the gentleman smiled at me and it seems that he made signals to call me. It wasn't the same person who followed me the other time. Now that I think about it, this is the third time. The first time one of the gentlemen invited me to the movies.

Of course I refused. This time I don't want to say anything to mother because she could be frightened.

# DECEMBER 31, 1945
# ROME

At midnight the new year begins.

If I think about the year of which today is the last day, many memories come to my mind. How many people, good and bad, have I met in the year 1945? How many new things have I learned? During this year a great transformation has taken place in me. I have known life from a new angle, but it is a very ugly angle. I have seen how great the goodness can be sometimes in people who are not related to us, and I have also seen how far the evil can sometimes go in people who are close relatives. I have seen how there is no justice in this world, and how useless it is to hope for it. Among the good people I can include the Cristofani family, who without any advantage has tried to help us as much as they were able to. This family includes three people: husband and wife and a daughter who is a teacher and a secretary in a "ginnasio." I know her because I have studied privately with her. When mother had to stay at Nettuno with Ralfi, they kept me with them for two months, and when I became ill with malaria, they took care of me better than if I had been their son. My teacher's father is an accountant, and he is as amiable and kind-hearted as he is intelligent. Her mother is a very kind-hearted and gentle person. In short, all this family is ... (I cannot find words to express what I would like to say). When mother needed money, they lent us several thousand lire, which mother hasn't yet been able to return to them, but they do not even ask for them, although they need them, because they know that mother cannot return the money to them for the time being. I have not yet met people like this in my life. I will always cherish a good memory of them, not of Signor Alexander though.

Let's now speak of that despicable person, Signor Alexander. He is exactly the opposite of the Cristofani family. In a few words: evil, without scruple, someone who does not hesitate to use any means to attain his aim. He is a criminal in gloves and a top-hat. Behind his smiling face hides a heart like . . . (as I didn't find words to describe the kindness of the Cristofanis, so do I not find words to describe the evil of this man).

## JANUARY 1, 1946 12:15 AM
## ROME

We have entered the new year. This is not a happy new year. What will the year 1946 bring us? Will we celebrate the next New Year's Day with father in America? Today Uncle Kuba has arrived from Holland. He has received a one month's leave but he spent eight days traveling, and another eight days must be taken into account for the return trip, so he will stay here for about two weeks.

Today Uncle Dolek and Aunt Ada moved into a room on via Udine. We will probably leave the apartment the day after tomorrow, and perhaps we will go live near Piazza Bologna.

## JANUARY 6, 1946
## ROME

Yesterday we moved into a room near Piazza Bologna, on via Polesine 8. Stairs B, Suite 19. Thus we have come to live very near Ralfi. However tonight we are going to get room and board at Signora Maria di Medici, via Udine 30, Stairs B, 48. The cause of this fast change is that mother has gotten sick again with neuralgia in this apartment, because it is very cold, and on the top floor.

On Tuesday I will start school again.

## JANUARY 6, 1946
## ROME

Tonight we slept in our new room.

## JANUARY 7, 1946
## ROME

Yesterday Mother left for Merano with Uncle Kuba.

## FEBRUARY 10, 1946
## ROME

Today is my birthday. I am turning fifteen. Today I cried when I thought about the present situation of my family. We have no news of papa. I find it impossible to believe that a person can have such a hard heart that when he has the possibility of providing a better life for us in America he doesn't do it.

# story
## *of a*
# jewish
# boy

# I.

SEPTEMBER 8TH, 1943!

This is a very distant date by now, but to me it seems only a few days ago.

It was a beautiful September day, one of those days that give the heart a sense of peace, but it was also a day that made the heart of many thousands of Italians bleed; many of these wounds have not yet healed.

September 8th! This date marks the tragic beginning of a terrible odyssey for many people, and so it was for us.

In the afternoon of that tragic day, I was in the garden of the house where I lived with my mother and my brother Raffaele. I was busy negotiating the exchange of some comic books with a school-mate. He suggested that we go to his house, which wasn't very far away, so that he could give me some illustrated albums in exchange for the comic books.

I agreed because I had nothing to do until my mother's return; she had gone to visit Raffaele in the hospital and therefore wouldn't be back for a couple of hours.

After having said goodbye to the friends who were with us, we started walking downhill. My friend and I were halfway there when we heard a voice shouting behind us, "Do you know what happened?!" We turned around and saw some children we knew in the garden of a nearby house.

That boy who had been the first to speak asked us again, "But don't you know that the armistice has been made with the English? They announced it on the radio a little while ago."

The news was so unexpected that neither I nor my friend believed it, and so we walked away, sure that those little boys were trying to make fun of us. I simply said," If it were true, it would be a wonderful thing," and then we didn't say any more about it.

A little later we arrived at the house where my friend lived, and he handed me the albums that he had promised me.

While we were talking, his mother came home and my friend told her about what we had heard in the street. The mother then said: "It's a strange thing, because I too heard something of the kind."

Soon after, I took my leave and went down to the street in order to go home. As I was walking, I thought again about what I had heard about the armistice, and in the end agreed that some of it might even be true. I made many conjectures as to what might happen if the hostilities had really ceased: in my thoughts I saw a tranquil life for myself in the future.

I certainly could not have imagined what really had happened. Thus I arrived at the house where I lived immersed in thought.

The idea of that armistice that I so wished for was so fixed in my head that I approached the window of a neighbor who lived on the ground floor and who owned a radio; right at that moment, he leaned out of the windowsill, and I asked him if he had heard on the radio if there were any news. He confirmed what I already knew.

I climbed the stairs and entered my house; I got myself an apple and began to read a comic book. After about an hour, the doorbell rang, and I imagined that it must be mother; while I went to open the door, I prepared myself to give her the good news. As I had imagined, it was in fact mother, corning back from the hospital where Raffaele was being taken care of I said to her right away, "Do you know that the armistice has been declared?"

Instead of showing surprise as I had imagined, mother answered in an indifferent tone, "Yes, I know." During dinner, we barely spoke about that event.

# II.

I woke up at dawn; it seemed to me to be the dawn of a new and better life. Two hours later, I had to partially change my mind: in fact, a new life was beginning, but not a better one.

After consuming a frugal breakfast, I went out with mother to visit my brother. When we were about to turn into the street in front of the hospital, I noticed something unusual; in fact, under the trees, there was a row of German tanks, as long as the entire street. We didn't know what had happened, but after we returned from the visit to Ralfi, we met an acquaintance who explained it to us. He told us that immediately after the armistice, the Germans had crossed the frontier and entered Italy; here, they had occupied the city and disarmed the Italian soldiers. He also told us that we had to leave Merano, because here all of the local Jews were known to the population, and so the SS would soon come to forcibly remove us from our house. We then asked him where he was going, but not even he had a destination.

After having received this less than joyful news, mother and I returned home.

While I was in the tram going to Maia Alta,[1] I noticed some things that previously I hadn't observed: quite a few civilians armed with muskets were walking on the street. An Italian who was near me explained that those guns had been taken away from Italian soldiers and given by the Germans to the local Nazis. The curious thing was that almost all of them carried three or four muskets on their shoulders.

---

1   Maia Alta: (*Obermais* in German) a leafy residential district of Merano on the south side of the Passirio river.

At a tram stop right in the middle of the Corso, there was a little scuffle inside the car. This is what had happened: a civilian armed with a rifle wanted to search the suitcase of an Italian man who had arrived just at that moment with the train; that Italian, completely frightened, tried to protest, and so the German snatched his suitcase and got off the tram. The owner of the suitcase also got off, and said that he wanted to go to city court to clear up the matter. Naturally, the German didn't want to hear about it, because he knew that he was wrong. I don't know how that affair ended up, because the tram was already starting to depart.

From the surrounding mountains one heard periodically the shots of a machine gun: it was a battalion of Italian riflemen who did not want to surrender to the Germans. In the evening I learned that those valorous men had been forced to surrender and that the Germans had penned them up in cattle wagons in order to deport them to Germany.

The tram had already almost arrived at Maia Alta, when I saw in the street an Italian soldier between two German civilians armed with three guns. The Germans carried him to their commander; that soldier had taken refuge in the mountains, but he had been taken by those two who were now leading him. As soon as he looked as if he was going to stop, one of the guardians pushed him on with his gun. Many Italian soldiers could have saved themselves from imprisonment by fleeing to the mountains, but they were hunted down by the local civilians who were familiar with the area, and who continued to search for them.

When we had gotten off the tram and were walking home, we met the Marchese Negroni, who was an acquaintance of ours. We asked him if he could perhaps give us advice on some way of leaving Merano in the shortest possible time; he suggested that we go to a boarding school in Turin headed by priests, and he said to us: "Maybe they will be able to help you in some way." We spoke a little while longer, and then mother said to him that if we were to leave today or tomorrow, we would leave him the keys of our house. He found no objection to this. After this, we took our leave, and he said to us that he would come by in the evening in order to find out whether we had come upon some way to leave.

Without returning home, we immediately went to the Palazzo Hotel, where the boarding school that the Marchese Negroni had mentioned was located. Mother asked to speak to the director, but he was not around, and so the reverend with whom my mother had spoken asked us to wait in the vestibule. We thus sat down in some armchairs, and awaited the return of the director, who had gone on an outing with some of the students.

After having waited about half an hour, we saw a band of students and certain priests enter. A few minutes later, we were received by the director. Mother explained our situation to him clearly and asked him whether he might be able to offer some help; he listened carefully then said to us: "I would very much like to help you, but I am afraid that it will not be that easy. Were it a question of just your son, the matter wouldn't be so difficult, because one of these days we are going to send the boys of this boarding school to Turin, and he could go with them under the pretext of being a student. For your sick son it is certainly not possible, because should the cars be stopped and checked by the Germans, there would be no pretext to explain his presence with us. For you Madame, it would be somewhat difficult, but if you were to dress up as a nun, it would be possible. I believe that the only feasible thing would be to leave your son here in the hospital, and then have him join you by means of an ambulance from Turin, considering that in Merano it is impossible to obtain one."

Mother explained to him that this was not possible, because she would absolutely never leave Ralfi in Merano. After this, we kindly thanked the·director, and left the Palazzo Hotel.

At first, we thought we could go home, but since it was already 12:50, and hence too late to begin cooking lunch, we decided to eat in a restaurant that was close by.

After having consumed a less-than-abundant repast, we went home. On the way, we ran into the Bonomi family's son, who was passing by on his bicycle; we asked him where his family was going, and he answered that they would be leaving by train for the outskirts of Bologna. Mother and I were very surprised that the railroads were still working, because that gentleman we'd run into in the morning, near the hospital, had said that the trains were not running for all destinations.

Once we were home, we thought long and hard about what might be the best city to go to. Finally we decided to go to Bologna, because the Istituto Rizzoli was there, which would have been perfect for Ralfi's illness.

Having made this decision, we left to go back to town once again. We had to take care of a few things; first of all make sure that the train was really departing, and in the case of an affirmative answer, go to Ralfi to inform him of our sudden departure; then buy the tickets for the trip from the C.I.T.

When we got to the station, we had to wait about ten minutes for the station master, because he was on the phone with Bolzano; when he had finished the communication, he turned to us and told us that the trains were working and that the one for Bologna was leaving the following day at 5:20 in the morning. We then asked him whether it was possible to bring trunks or crates. He said no, it was not.

Having obtained this information, we went to Ralfi. My brother was somewhat surprised to learn about our hurried departure.

We weren't able to linger long with Ralfi, because it was already 5:45 and we still had to go to the C.I.T. to get our tickets, and that office closed at 6:30.

By 6:15, we had already gotten the tickets at the C.I.T., and since we had nothing else to do in the city, we took the tram to go home. In the stretch of road between the tram stop and the building where we lived, we ran into Madame Imlaufer, who had an antique store in

Merano. We spoke briefly with her, and in this way learned that she too was leaving for Bologna, where she had a niece. Before we said goodbye, we came to the agreement that we would go with her to the train station the following day. Since she had spoken with a porter to carry the luggage, this same fellow could've carried our suitcases as well.

Having arrived at home, we ate a light meal, and soon after having finished, the Marchese Negroni arrived. Mother explained to him what would be the most important things to save. After about an hour, he left, and said that he would come the following day to take the keys and to take us to the station. He also added that he would phone the Red Cross, so that they would send an ambulance to the hospital the following day at 5:10.

When the Marchese Negroni left, mother began to put our stuff in the suitcases. We decided that we would bring only two suitcases and a hatbox, because at the station they had told us that we couldn't bring either trunks or crates. After all, we weren't sure that we could bring our suitcases. Mother had to leave many useful things, because they were in the dining room, where we couldn't turn on the lights. I went to sleep while mother stayed up packing.

When I was in bed, I thought again about the events of that day, and the scenes of bullying and cowardice that I had seen replayed themselves in my mind.

The moonlight fell onto the floor of the room; every so often, a gunshot broke the nocturnal silence!

What would await us the next day?

# III.

It often happens to me that when I know I must get up early in the morning, there is no need for me to be woken up, and that actually I get up before the due time. This is how it went on September 10th, the day we had to leave for Bologna at five twenty. I woke up at about four, and with surprise noted that mother had not gone to bed and had stayed up all night packing and preparing the crates that the Marchese Negroni might be able to save at Madame Weinhart's house.

Not long after I had washed and dressed, the Marchese Negroni arrived. I ran to Madame Imlaufer, who did not live so far away, in order to ask whether she and her niece, who accompanied her aunt to Bolzano, were ready.

I found them already prepared to leave, and the porter was carrying their suitcases downstairs. Soon after, we went to our house; I ran to bring the suitcases down. It was not very easy to arrange them on the porter's cart, because Madame Imlaufer had a lot of luggage. When finally everything was ready, we set off towards the station.

The streets were deserted; only some earlybirds could be seen. It was still dark; and the first lights of dawn were barely visible. One could still see a couple of stars. At ten past five, we arrived at the station.

The Marchese Negroni went to the hospital in order to have the administrative office give him the piece of paper with which Ralfi would have been able to leave the hospital. After a few minutes, he ran back, and told us that the ambulance had not yet arrived: we didn't know what to do, because the train was leaving in a few moments. Then mother ran to the station master to beg him to make the train wait a few minutes. Finally the ambulance arrived and Ralfi was put in the train; it was not an easy thing, because Ralfi was in a cast that went from his chest to the ankle of his right leg. A number of maneuverings were necessary in order to put him in the compartment. At thirty minutes past five, the train departed: there had been a ten-minute delay because of Ralfi.

I leaned out of the window: the train was passing the iron bridge over the Passirio River. After a few minutes, it was in the countryside. My eyes bid farewell to Merano. When was I to see my native city again?

The train sped through the orchards; the apple and pear trees bent under the weight of their fruit. On certain trees, there were so many beautiful red apples that there were supports so the branches would not break.

I had always wanted to travel, but on that day I would have rather stayed home. Ralfi also tried to lean out of the window, but every so often he had to lie down because he grew too tired.

Soon we could no longer see Merano, and around us we could see nothing but fields and, a little bit farther off, mountains. Every so often, an early-rising farmer would stop his work to watch the train speed by before his eyes. On the mountains one could see some villages. When was I to see those mountains and those fields again? These questions remained without answers.

An hour after the train had left Merano, the city of Bolzano came into view. In the distance, I could see the rubble of the recent bombing. This was something new for me, since I had never seen an aerial attack, and even less its effects.

The train was by this point close to the bridge over the Adige, when it slowed down to stop at a small station. At the station were some ashen-faced Germans, with pistols and machine guns slung over their shoulders. Two of them boarded the train. Soon word spread that the Germans were searching the train for two Italian soldiers who, in Merano, had escaped the Germans, and whom they thought were on the train.

We were afraid that the Germans would ask us for our documents, because had they done this they would've seen that we were Jewish, and the matter would've ended up badly. Luckily they only had men show their identity cards; nonetheless, I got a chill down my spine when they came into our compartment.

When they had gone, I leaned out the window, and was surprised to see that some Germans were searching under the train for people hiding there or between the train's bumpers. An hour later, the train was finally able to take off again. The Germans hadn't found those Italian soldiers they'd been searching for, but instead found about ten men without valid documentation.

The train went quite slowly over the bridge, because the tracks had just been repaired after the bombing damages.

The train let out a sharp whistle, and pulled into the Bolzano station panting like a dog after a long run.

Before it had stopped, I leaned out of the train car to call a porter. While I lowered the suitcase from the train window, mother went to call the Red Cross militia men in order to have them take Ralfi off the train on a stretcher. While Ralfi and the suitcases were being led across the tracks to the platform from which the train to Bologna left, mother and I went through the underpass.

When we arrived on the platform, neither Ralfi nor the suitcases were there. However, it didn't take long for them to join us.

The train for Bologna, the one that came from the Brenner, normally would not have taken long to come, but the loudspeaker of the station announced that the BrennerRome train would have a one-hour delay. We set about waiting patiently. Ralfi tossed about on his stretcher, which was indeed not very soft, while mother sat on a suitcase, given that there were no benches in these surroundings.

I had no inclination to stay put for an hour, so I took a little tour around the station.

I had just stepped away from my family, when a scene that was unworthy of the twentieth century, which according to some people ought to be civilized, appeared before my own brown eyes. It was this: A train composed of sealed box-cars which usually carry luggage, goods, and cattle. This time the goods were quite different. In fact, the cars were carrying human freight! It might seem unbelievable but I can assure you that I saw it with my own eyes in the middle of the 20th century. I'll explain with more details. If you have ever seen a box-car, you will recall that it only has one window covered with a thick metal screen. This is the type of freight train I saw. Besides that, the doors were leadsealed. I realize I haven't told you who those wretched people were, locked up in this way. They were Italian soldiers that the Germans had taken prisoner in their barracks, and now were being deported to death camps.

Besides this, I saw that some people were afraid of the German with the face of a bandit who walked back and forth on the platform in front of the train, and who held a loaded machine gun under his arm like an umbrella or a walking stick.

I asked a bystander why those people clutched the train windows (if they deserve that name), and what those people who hurried toward the box-car were doing. The gentleman kindly explained to me in great detail: "These prisoners are trying to give the addresses of their families so that those kind persons may inform their families of their situation. Furthermore those gentlemen and ladies were also trying to secretly give them apples or a piece of bread (secretly because otherwise that soldier would be more than willing to make the gift of a bullet in the belly to whomever he saw giving a piece of old bread to one of those poor men who had not eaten for many days)." This gentleman had hardly finished giving me this explanation, when from the train leapt a scream that had in it something tragic, as tragic were the proffered words: "There's a dead person! There's a dead person! Take him away!" The last words had such an imploring tone that all those present were moved by it - all except one person, that is, the German who continued to walk back and forth, unperturbed, rhythmically stamping his hobnailed boots on the stone platform. His heart was certainly hard as that stone.

I returned to where mother was and we were hurrying toward the train windows, on which leaned many of those poor soldiers who were guilty of no crime but that of being Italian. Then these people quickly moved away while. I waited impatiently for the train, because I wanted to get away from that place which had, by then, become revolting to me.

After a long two-hour wait, the train finally came. It was not easy to board it.

One couldn't even imagine getting Ralfi on it through the door, since the corridor was so crowded that one could not even pass without a stretcher. So two members of the Red Cross militia got into the train car, and by forcefully elbowing their way succeeded in opening a passage as far as the first compartment, and here they asked some young ladies to kindly get up, because they had to put a sick person there. Having done this, the Red Cross people leaned out of the window and told the other two people who were standing next to Ralfi to lift the stretcher up to the height of the window. It wasn't easy because Ralfi isn't all that light. Besides, there was also the danger that he could fall, because the stretcher was being handed inside at an angle through the window, given that the latter was very narrow. Throughout the operation, mother and I held our breaths. Ralfi was also afraid. The suitcases passed through the same way Ralfi had, and the two of us also entered, but not through the train window.

We had just joined Ralfi in the train car, when the train began to move. The trip was quite monotonous. Every so often, we saw long convoys of German motor vehicles beaten-up and badly damaged. Upon seeing such wreckage, one immediately understood the horrible losses suffered by the Germans.

We passed Verona and Trento, and toward seven at night we were in the vicinity of Bologna. The region looked completely different from that which we had seen up to this moment. As far as the eye could see, there were no mountains, and at the end of that endless plain a great red ball, the solar sphere, rapidly descending, descending, descending and finally disappearing as though swallowed by the earth. It was a stirring sight that neither I nor Ralfi had ever seen before. We asked a fellow traveler from Bologna about the bombings, and he gave us some explanations. In addition, he told us that we wouldn't be arriving in the main station but that, on the contrary, the train had to stop in a little station before Bologna because, further on, the tracks were pulled up by the recent air raid. Not long after, in fact, the train slowed down and stopped in front of a station, where before the war surely not even a freight train would have stopped, but now had acquired a certain degree of importance.

Mother got off the train in order to find out whether it was possible to obtain a stretcher. In no time came mother, stretcher, station master, and another man who had offered to help. In that modest station there was even a waiting room, and we went there for the time being. Do not imagine a large elegant room with all the comforts. In that place there were not even the most necessary things. But I want to describe to you, as best I can, this place I am calling a waiting room.

This was a room that, besides its walls, had nothing else. There were a few people who had been waiting for the train for who knows how long. They were sitting on their suitcases, and some of them slept on the floor. The dirty floor was covered in fruit peels, flyers, and newspapers. We made do as best as we could in a corner that seemed a bit more decent than the rest.

After having settled down in this way, we went to try to find out how we could go with Ralfi to the Istituto Rizzoli. The station master told us that in order to obtain an ambulance, we needed the permission of the German headquarters, which was stationed quite a few kilometers from the station; he furthermore told us that the curfew at Bologna was 9 p.m., and it was almost that time; although she was afraid, mother thought it best to go to the German headquarters but she had to abandon this thought because the curfew was imminent, and if the Germans saw someone walking around after nine, they didn't think twice before shooting.

We had nearly resigned ourselves to spending the night in that dirty station, but this time again fortune was in our favor. Help came to us in the form of a man who was riding his bicycle to Bologna.

He agreed to go to the German command post to beg the Germans to call an ambulance, so that they could come and pick us up, because only they were able to use the telephone.

This being accomplished, we returned to Ralfi, who was impatiently waiting to know what we had concluded.

We remained for a while longer in that big room, but then we decided to go out, both because there was so much filth, and because that filth did not emit an odor that was pleasing to our nostrils.

With the aid of the station master, I brought Ralfi out into the open air; at first, we were happy enough to be outside, but as soon as it started getting dark, another difficulty befell us, not lesser than that which had induced us to leave the waiting room, and to be precise, those annoying little beasts called "mosquitoes" came and bit us everywhere. Ralfi was the worst off of us all, because, unable to move, he was the favorite prey of those animals. In order to help him swat them away, mother and I took turns fanning a handkerchief in front of his face. When it was mother's turn, I stepped aside to take a little stroll, and I entered the office of the station master: this was a room furnished with few pieces of furniture and one or two framed pictures; in the center of the room, besides the station master, there were other men who were talking amongst themselves. These were some of the Italian soldiers who had fled from the army on September 8th, the day of the armistice. They were in civilian garb given to them by the peasants so they could flee unobserved. During the day, they stayed hidden in the fields, and at night they walked on foot in order to rejoin their families in northern Italy. They were eating some grapes that they had stolen during the day in the fields in order to alleviate their hunger. They offered me a bunch, and I accepted it and brought some of it to mother and Ralfi.

After a while, in the station master's room, those men were about to leave. I thought: who knows if they will return? Maybe they will end up like those wretched men I had seen at the Bolzano station. In my heart, I wished them to return safe and sound to their families.

After they left, I paced up and down in the station, when at a certain moment I heard the sound of a car approaching. As soon as it came around the corner, I could see it clearly. It was a German car coming right up to the station. A vague sense of fear came upon me, because I thought that maybe they were looking for us. The car stopped almost in front of me and three German soldiers and one Italian interpreter got off.

As I had suspected, they asked for the sick boy, and I answered the interpreter that I would immediately call mother. After a while I returned with mother; she. was quite frightened. The interpreter told her that they wanted to take Ralfi to the Istituto Forlanini with their car. Mother answered them in Italian (because she did not want to show them that she knew German) that this was not possible because an ambulance was necessary. The interpreter translated mother's words for the Germans. Then the sergeant, with whom the interpreter had spoken, said that they wanted to administer an injection. When mother heard these words, even before the interpreter had translated them, she grew pale; I was amazed by this, but right away I realized the reason, and in fact mother had grown pale when she had heard that they wanted to administer an injection to Ralfi, because in Merano it had been rumored that in Germany the Germans injected sick Jews with poison in order to get rid of them. The Germans with whom we spoke certainly did not intend to administer an injection of this sort, but mother's fear for Ralfi had led her to see things as worse than they actually were. She in fact immediately began to say that there was no need for this, because Ralfi's was not an illness he had suffered during the trip, but was a long-standing illness. While speaking, she said a few words in German, and I feared that she might betray herself, but luckily mother quickly calmed herself and showed the Germans that Ralfi was in a cast, and that an ambulance was necessary. They left and promised they would call the Italian Red Cross so that they would bring an ambulance.

When finally the roar of the car moved away, mother and I breathed a sigh of relief.

A few hours passed, and we thought that the Germans hadn't phoned the Red Cross, and we were resigned to spending the night in the station, when around about midnight, we heard the sound of a car. I ran out to see, and in fact a car was approaching. When it was quite close to the station, I recognized that it was an ambulance. I immediately imagined that it was coming for us, and in fact I had not been deceived. A doctor got out of the cab and asked to see the sick person; I brought him to my brother.

A little later, the doctor, myself, and the nurse carried Ralfi to the ambulance, and we put him onto the stretcher, and mother and I took a seat beside him. Soon after, the car was racing on the road towards Bologna.

The road was lit up by the full moon.

We were already on the outskirts of the city when an "Alt" resounded, and the car stopped. I looked out of the narrow window, and saw some Germans, with their machine guns poised, stationed at the fork in the road. It was a check point at the entrance of the city. As soon as the soldiers saw the Red Cross vehicle, they immediately let it pass; the trip continued without further interruption until the Istituto Rizzoli. Having arrived in front of the large building, the car stopped in front of a large door, and the driver honked his horn. Some minutes passed, and finally the door opened without a sound, and the car entered a large room. As soon as it had stopped, I got off and looked around this place that was new for me.

The place where we had entered was an enormous room, as high as the whole building, and the vaulted ceiling was supported by four gigantic columns. Mother too got off and went towards the doorman, who was standing behind a semicircular table in a corner of the room.

The doorman called the on-call doctor, and mother explained to him Ralfi's disease. That doctor then called for a nurse, asking her to bring a stretcher with her; furthermore, he asked what room with three beds was free. Once he had heard her answer, he went to see Ralfi.

In the meantime, a nurse came with a stretcher. It was a stretcher mounted on four wheels, such that one person alone could carry him. When Ralfi was placed atop it, and mother had paid the driver of the ambulance, the nurse led us to the elevator. I thought that it wasn't possible to enter the elevator with the stretcher, but when the elevator opened, I saw that I had been mistaken; in fact this elevator was so large that two beds could comfortably fit inside of it. We went down to the first floor and walked down a long, large corridor; having arrived at the end, we took a right down another corridor, and entered the fifth room on the left. This was quite a large room, with three beds on which there were only mattresses. The nurse who had accompanied us went to get the blankets. When she returned, we were surprised that she hadn't brought the sheets.

She told us that this night we needed to do without them because the person in charge of the hospital linen was not at work that day. This organization surprised us quite a bit.

As soon as the nurse had made the bed, Ralfi was put in, and soon both mother and myself followed suit.

Before falling asleep, for a long time I thought about everything that had happened during the day. What unforeseen change had taken place in our habitual life.

That sad day was the beginning of a chain of other horrible days.

# IV.

Notwithstanding the fact that I had gone to sleep so late, I awoke at around eight thirty.

While still half asleep, I saw the sun's rays on the floor, filtering through the halfclosed blinds.

At first, I thought that I was still in my little room in Merano. It seemed as if I had only dreamed of many strange and awful things. But soon, this fog cleared itself from my eyes and my mind. Only then did I realize that I hadn't dreamed, but instead had lived that which I thought was a terrible dream.

Mother too was already awake and it didn't take long for Ralfi to awaken.

Once I had gotten up and washed myself, because breakfast had not yet been brought, I went into the garden. I went down in the large elevator, and when I was down in the lobby, I asked a nurse which way I should go in order to get into the garden. Having gotten directions, I exited from a large door and found myself in an enclosed garden surrounded by the hospital building. There were some paths surrounded by flower beds, that had clearly not been tended for quite a long time. Walking along one of those paths, which was slightly larger than the rest, I immediately arrived at another large door, parallel to the one I had just come out of. Having passed through this one, I found myself in the garden. It was a large park.

On the borders and in the center there were some gigantic pine trees. In the center, was a large flower bed, which at one time must have been covered with green grass and sweet-smelling flowers, and was now trodden and unkempt. A few people were lying down on reclining chairs to sun themselves, because it was a beautiful day. Other people walked with crutches on the gravel.

I walked a little bit and stopped in a small semicircular esplanade surrounded by chestnut trees.

There were two benches on either side and a wooden bench on the side of the escarpment. On the bench on the right a man was sunning himself, I have just said that there was a small slope, surrounded by dry chestnut leaves; a boy was gathering horse chestnuts that the wind had shaken from the trees. Every so often, he shook a low branch with a stick in order to make other chestnuts fall.

At the end of that small escarpment, the paved street led to Bologna.

At that moment, a doctor's Topolino[2] passed by quickly, because it had a red cross on the back window. In those days, Germans confiscated all of the cars, and let only doctors keep them. Raising my eyes, I saw Bologna's glorious panorama. From the point where I was, I could dominate the city's entirety with my gaze.

It seemed as though "La Dotta"[3] was waking right then; the sun was breaking up the morning fog and shone on the large white buildings. The massive structure of the Gothic duomo towered above the city's other buildings. I could also clearly see the two towers of the Asinelli.

A large white edifice caught my eyes; because I couldn't tell what it was, I asked the person who was seated on the bench. He told me that that modern white building was the headquarters of the newspaper *Il Resto del Carlino*.

I looked a little longer at the vista, and then retraced my steps.

---

2   Topolino: literally "Little Mouse," this was the nickname for the first Fiat 500, so called because it was one of the smallest cars in the world. In production from 1937 to 1955.

*Topolino* is also the Italian name of Mickey Mouse, first appearing in Italy in 1932.

3   La Dotta: literally "the learned," this was the nickname for Bologna's university, the oldest in Europe.

Instead of immediately returning to the room, I took a stroll about the park once more. On one side of the garden, I came to a slight elevation of the ground, and I walked up a few stone steps. In that place, there were some greenhouses, and a gardener who was transplanting some small plants.

I realized that I had stayed a bit too long and thus I decided to return. But instead of retracing my steps from whence I had come, I went around the building and entered through the main door.

When I arrived at our room, breakfast had already been brought and mother and Ralfi had already begun to eat.

Mother told me that we were moving to another room, bigger and sunnier.

Having finished breakfast we immediately started moving out.

Our new room was opposite the other and the window was overlooking the small courtyard through which I had passed while I was going to the garden.

Mother had just arranged our things a bit when the medical team came around. The head of the Istituto Rizzoli examined Ralfi and told the nurse to have an x-ray taken; he also said that the cast which had been made at the hospital in Merano was very bad because it was too thick and too heavy, and therefore on the following day they would make a new one.

Once the examination was over and the doctors had left, Ralfi wanted to go into the garden.

A nurse brought a sort of little bed mounted on four wheels and placed Ralfi on it. I myself put him in the elevator and took him to the garden and showed him the panorama of Bologna.

Then at lunchtime, around one, we returned to the room.

During lunch mother and I decided to go to the city in the afternoon to pay a visit to an acquaintance.

In fact, after the meal we went down. Coming out of the large lobby we crossed the large square in front of the building, and went down about twenty steep stone steps, and arrived under a small canopy where other people were also waiting for the bus.

Shortly afterwards a bus went by, but it wasn't going to Bologna. We had to wait until it circled around the square in front of the church, which stood next to the Istituto Rizzoli, and came back afterwards downhill. All of this didn't take longer than five minutes. The trip to the city took about fifteen minutes.

We got off in Piazza Cavour, right in front of the Banca d'Italia.

The street where our acquaintance lived was not very far. In order to get there we had to go down via Farini and then via Barberia.

Piazza Cavour was surrounded by arcades. The vaults were painted with frescoes portraying battle scenes from centuries ago.

Going along via Farini, we could see the damage caused by the latest air raids: torn out and twisted store shutters. Not a pane of glass was intact, at least of those that were there before the bombings, and the new ones were encased in strips of paper, so that the pressure waves would not damage them.

Of a large building there was nothing left save four walls; of the interior there was no trace.

In other parts of the city there were houses that hadn't completely collapsed, and then one could read these words written on a sign planted in the ground: "ATTENTION! DANGER OF COLLAPSE! STAY AWAY!"

The most important road arteries were full of holes caused by fragments of incendiary bombs. The cars proceeded in a "ZIG-ZAG" in order to avoid the holes. The walls of the buildings were blackened by fires. Elsewhere in some corner of the street, there was a heap of rubble, and here also one could read on a piece of wood these laconic words:" ATTENTION! UNEXPLODED BOMB!"

Our acquaintance lived on a little street and I noticed that it had been spared by the bombardment.

At about four we went back to the Istituto. In the meantime Ralfi had had the x-rays taken and they had cut the cast in half. While mother was putting the things that were in the suitcase into the closet, I played checkers with Ralfi.

After dinner I read a book and went to bed early.

# V.

The following day they made a nice cast for Ralfi, a lot thinner than the one made in the Merano hospital.

Days went by without anything important happening. I took Ralfi to the garden almost every day.

On the twenty-third of the same month, that is of September, mother left for Merano. Mother had decided this because she wanted to see what had been saved of our things, and to see what could still be saved. I will therefore follow this trip, which by a miracle did not end tragically.

The day before her departure, and precisely on the twenty-second, mother had gone with me to the Stazione Centrale (in the meantime the tracks damaged by the air raids had been repaired, and the trains could already reach Bologna directly) to inquire when and at what time the trains to Bolzano were leaving. Having gotten the information she wanted, mother bought a ticket and the following morning at seven thirty she went back to the station to set out on her trip. She had an empty suitcase with her (empty, because mother was hoping to bring back to Bologna some of our things that Marchese Negroni perhaps had managed to salvage).

She immediately boarded the train, although the train was to leave more than an hour and a half later. It was already extremely crowded and one couldn't even think of finding a seat. Those who were seated had certainly been in the train since the night before.

More people were arriving all the time, and soon one stood so cramped that one couldn't move a step.

In those days there was a lot of coming and going because many soldiers had left their uniforms to don civilian clothes when the armistice had broken out, and most of those were trying to rejoin their families.

At the moment of departure there were many people, and in the most unimaginable places, so much so that someone who hasn't seen it would have a hard time believing it.

The people were hanging in bunches from the doors of the cars. Not a few fell during the trip, and those who did not get squashed by the heavy wheels of the train could be called fortunate.

There were also those who sat on the roof with a great risk of suffocating from the smoke or of being electrocuted by high voltage wires.

The most fought-for place was between the bumpers of the cars. If someone sitting in that place lost his balance he could be certain of getting pulled to pieces in between the tracks. In those times railroad accidents happened very often.

But let's finally go back to the main subject of the story. Mother had to get off at the Verona station because the train was going to Milan and not Bolzano. Because that same evening there was no connection for continuing on, mother had to resign herself to spending the night at the station. There was neither a seat on any bench nor in the waiting room, because there were people there who had already been waiting for the train for several days, and therefore she had to sit on the suitcase she had with her and wait for the rising of the day.

The station had a miserable aspect. Exhausted people were lying on the cold asphalt. When the loudspeaker announced the departure or the arrival of a train, the heads of those people would lift up, the better to listen. Then there was a swarming of people hurrying to reach the train cars.

The others sighed with disappointment and then dropped heavily back on their hard beds.

At times those who were going to catch the train would stumble onto those who were lying down, and then a curse could be heard, followed by words of apology.

Finally, there appeared on the horizon a clear streak, which grew wider and wider. One by one the stars slowly faded away, and the moon also disappeared to give its place up to the half-hearted morning sun, and, for all, the longed-for day came.

Finally, the train to Bolzano also arrived, and mother got on it. At Bolzano, one had to change trains again for Merano. At noon, mother arrived in this city, the destination of the trip.

As soon as she got off the train car, she saw Signora Gruner (Umlauf) coming

towards her, and noticed that her face showed surprise, amazement, and almost fear.

Not for a second could mother have imagined that the cause of this was the mere fact of her appearance. However, from Signora Gruner's words she saw that it was precisely this that was the cause of it.

In fact, this is what she said: "Madame, why on earth did you come to Merano? Don't you know that you are risking your life? Don't you know that all the Jews of this city have been deported by the S.S.? If you get caught you can be sure you won't see your children again. Listen to me! Catch the first train and leave. I cannot continue speaking with you because if someone speaks with or helps the Jews he gets shot instantly. Go back, for God's sake, if you don't want to end up like so many others in the death camps in Poland."

She said this hurriedly and in a whisper, and as soon as she finished she hurried away.

It is difficult, almost impossible, to describe the thoughts that passed through mother's mind after that encounter.

It seemed to her as if everything was falling, everything was collapsing around her. Everything had happened so quickly that she couldn't convince herself of it all.

When she was finally able to organize her thoughts, she started going toward the exit. At that point it felt as if she had been standing there for hours. She tried to strike a calm attitude, as it seemed to her that everyone's eyes were fixed on her; that everyone would go and betray her.

Thoughts went rapidly through her mind. It seemed to her as if she had been already captured and sealed in a boxcar to be deported. A shiver ran down her spine.

Then she thought about Signora Gruner's words and remembered that Signora Gruner had told her to leave immediately. She then went to the information window and asked when the first train to Bolzano was. She thus learned that there was one leaving only in the late afternoon, and therefore mother had to spend many hours in Merano. Where should she go?

First, she thought of going to Lana, a village near Merano, but soon she abandoned this idea, because along the way she might run into some inhabitant of Merano, and therefore would risk being denounced. Another reason was that she might run into the Germans, who would be likely to ask for her documents.

At the end she decided to hide in a small park to the left of the station. It was a small square space, surrounded by a tall hedge, such that from the outside whoever was inside could not be seen. This garden was almost always little frequented because it was in a sparsely populated neighborhood.

So, mother entered and saw that no one was there. She sat down on one of the benches, having left her suitcase at the luggage deposit office of the station. After sitting for over an hour, she felt the need to move. At first, she paced far and wide across the park.

Now and then the silence was pierced by the hoot of a train arriving or departing. Mother sat down again, but soon got up and walked out of the garden through a little street.

A little boy was playing in the middle of the street, making sand cakes. A little further away a woman was sitting on a bench, a bucket and a scraper next to her: evidently, she was the nanny of the boy who was playing. This woman was sewing. Mother sat down on the same bench where the woman was sitting.

Time passed but every minute felt like a century. For no one do the hours pass as slowly as for those who wait.

About ten minutes had gone by since mother had sat down when an officer of the Italian army came to sit on the same bench. He appeared to be absorbed in thoughts that were not light. Soon he did not keep them in his mind any longer and started to speak, not directly to the people present, but evidently with the intention of making himself heard by them. In fact, he began to talk to himself out loud.

This was his soliloquy: "What terrible times these are! It's an impossible situation! I find myself in an ugly situation. I don't know what to do! Must I present myself to the German headquarters or not."

Perhaps he would have continued, but evidently he was annoyed that no one was paying too much attention to him. In fact, in those times everyone had enough of their own troubles on their minds, without listening to those of others. He then turned to my mother and asked her: "Are you from Merano?"

She said she was, but immediately regretted it, because that officer might ask her on what street she lived. He could perhaps be a German spy, she thought. Luckily the officer did not ask her anything else and soon he left. He wasn't a spy at all, but fear had made mother see a non-existent danger, among so many real ones.

Shortly afterwards, however, she ran a really serious risk. In fact, a cyclist passed, coming from Lana. Mother recognized him as a well-known Nazi from Merano. He certainly would not hesitate to denounce her to the Germans. Luckily, he passed in front of her without seeing her, but mother became as pale as a washed-out rag, and when she saw him turn onto the main road at the end of the street, she sighed with relief.

Not long afterwards she got up and went toward the station. She was walking slowly because the departure was still a long time away. She climbed the large staircases of the station, claimed her suitcase and bought a ticket to Bologna.

As the train was already in the station mother got on it and waited nervously for its departure to Bolzano. Shortly afterwards people started to get in. The station master shouted: "All aboard! The train is leaving." And when all the doors were closed, finally the station master waved the flag and the train let out a long whistle and left puffing.

I won't describe this voyage, but I will only say that once mother had left Bolzano she already felt very relieved.

The train from Verona pulled into the station of Bologna on the morning of September twenty-fifth. Mother got off. She took the trolley car to Piazza Cavour, where she should have caught the bus that would have taken her to the Istituto Rizzoli. But on the trolley car she ran into Signora Imlaufer's niece.

At first, upon seeing mother, she seemed not to recognize her, but when she was closer to her and realized that it was really her, she looked at mother as one looks at a ghost, a person raised from the dead. Finally, she said these words: "Why, Signora Bermann, is it really you?! I cannot quite believe it. We all thought you were dead. A student coming from Merano told us the terrible things that happened in that city, and we thought you had been already deported or shot dead. Come to our house to tell us how you escaped. If I tell people I have seen you alive, I wouldn't be believed."

Mother went home with Signora Imlaufer's niece. When she arrived at their house there were new displays of surprise. As much as mother wanted to come back to me and to Ralfi, she was forced to tell all the details of her trip.

Finally at around nine forty-five, she took the trolley car, and, once arrived in Piazza Cavour, put herself on the tram and here we will leave her for the time being.

# VI.

During mother's absence I became acquainted with a few boys who were staying at the Istituto Rizzoli. Some were hospitalized, others were accompanying a sick relative, as was the case with me.

One of those who was hospitalized had a hand that was paralyzed. I asked him how that accident had happened, and he told me his painful adventure.

Here it is, briefly explained: He was a sixteen-year-old boy who lived in a small town near Bari. It was summer. The sea was only a few kilometers away. Every now and then, actually quite often, this boy went swimming. In order to get to the beach, he had to go through a small station.

One beautiful morning, the sky was clear and cloudless; the day promised to be clear and warm. The boy decided to go swimming. He happily took to the dusty road. He arrived at the station. Here the accident happened! While he was crossing the tracks, a long train of cattle cars was shunting to couple up with two detached cars on a dead-end track. He was about to cross precisely that track. At that moment, with a dull clanking noise, the train had coupled up with the two cars. If that boy had taken a step forward his body would have been crushed. His right hand instead got mangled between the bumpers.

He screamed. Many people rushed to him. The train was disconnected from the bumpers of the cars. He was taken to the emergency room. The hand was not bleeding, but he could not move it. The nerve no longer worked.

He was taken to the hospital. At the end, after a few months and many experiments without results, he was sent to the Istituto Rizzoli. Here his nerve was operated on. He showed me where he had been cut. There were fourteen stitches. From the wrist almost to the elbow.

Every day he had to undergo light electric shocks on his hand, in order for the nerve to wake up again. Day after day the shocks reached greater intensity. He was already able to move some fingers a bit. In a few days it was to be put in a cast.

On the morning of September twenty-fifth, at about nine thirty, I was strolling through the corridors in the company of the boy of whom I have just spoken.

We were speaking of this and that when we were met by a young lady who was staying at the Istituto Rizzoli with her mother, who had a problem with both of her legs.

She turned to my friend, whom she knew, to ask him to go downtown to buy a spool of cotton. He said he would go, and asked me if I wanted to go with him.

I thought for a while, and finally decided to go with him, since I had almost nothing to do, and I wanted to get to know Bologna better. Five minutes later, we were going down the stone steps, and then we were at the trolley stop.

From some people who were waiting we learnt that the uphill trolley had not come yet, and therefore we must wait five minutes. Finally, it arrived. Almost noiselessly. It stopped and a few people got off. To my great amazement, I saw mother get off as well. I ran toward her and hugged her.

It was a real surprise for me, as I did not expect her to come back so soon. I apologized to my friend for not being able to go with him, and so, with mother, retraced my way back to Istituto Rizzoli. I took the suitcase she was carrying, and was very surprised that it was empty.

When we arrived in the room, mother hugged and kissed Ralfi, and then started to tell us about her trip. Ralfi and I, while she was telling her story, were dismayed in hearing of the risk run by mother. Every now and then I would interrupt her to ask her a question.

Shortly afterwards I left the room and went down the corridor. When I arrived in front of the large window I leaned out and looked in the garden. It was a clear, limpid day. I could see only some tiny white clouds, which looked like wads of cotton-wool dropped by a mysterious giant during his voyage.

I thought back to mother's trip, and reconstructed in my mind some scenes of her story. I was much absorbed in my thoughts, when my ear perceived the drone of an airplane. I leaned out the windowsill trying to make out the aircraft. It must have been very high. From the noise it sounded like an American reconnaissance aircraft. Light fog prevented me from seeing it. Some people in the meantime had gathered near the window also trying to make it out. Now and then one could hear that it went farther, and then it returned. Evidently it was circling above Bologna at a very high altitude.

After about ten minutes the noise faded definitely away, and those people were already leaving when a whistle was heard, as if from a siren, but it was similar to a balloon deflating.[4]

Shortly afterwards another whistle was heard, like the preceding one. Some people shouted: "The alarm! The alarm! Let's run to the shelter!" In a second, everyone was running through the corridors. Some were running this way, some that way. Some were running to the shelter, others were going to the rooms downstairs to get the relatives who were unable to walk. A few women were already starting to cry, screaming: "Oh God! Oh God!"

I ran to the room, to mother and Ralfi. I wasn't at all frantic, as so many others were. Perhaps someone reading this would find it

4    As we learn a few days later, it had been precisely a balloon, which had been dropped by American aircraft to warn the population and deflated in the air.

hard to believe, but it was really this way because I had never seen nor heard a bombardment; it was quite different than the alarms that followed this one.

When I came into the room, I found Ralfi who was already on the wheelchair. I took the chair and led it out of the room. I pushed it while running. Behind me mother came. The corridor was full of beds and deckchairs. While I was running I heard the airplanes passing above the Istituto. I reached the elevator. There was some room left in it and I placed Ralfi inside. I also wanted to get in, with mother, but there was no room. Mother and I ran downstairs. I was running down three steps at a time, and in a moment I arrived in front of the elevator door.

Meanwhile, one could hear the bombs falling. There was a thick hail of shells. The German anti-aircraft artillery was silent. The windows were shaking. People were running downstairs in the direction of the shelter. The noise of the explosions was mixed with the crashing of the beds on the first floor.

Mother and I were waiting for the elevator. The seconds seemed like hours. Terribly frightened, we realized that the elevator wasn't coming at all. In that tragic moment I sensed that something must have happened to the electricity. Without wasting a second, I ran to the first floor. I was climbing the stairs three steps at a time. I had almost arrived at the top of the staircase when mother shouted: "Come down! Come down! If we must die, let's die together, come down!"

I told her to stay calm. Other people as well, who had gone through more than one bombardment, shouted at her to keep calm. In the meantime one could hear the dull crash of the shells. The glass panes were shaking. I arrived at the first floor. People were running here and there. The corridor became more and more cluttered with beds. Cries could be heard. A few women and some small children were crying. There was a terrible chaos. When the waves of bombers passed above the building, women took their head in their hands, desperate. Others were praying.

I ran toward the elevator door. I grabbed both handles with my hands, and with all my strength tried to open them. I tried one, two, three times, but the mechanical force was greater than the human. Finally even mother came upstairs, and then we learnt that they had opened the elevator door from the other side of the corridor. We ran in that direction. We found that the elevator door was wide open, and that the elevator itself was about fifty centimeters lower than the corridor. A few nurses were carrying Ralfi out, and they made him stand. Shortly afterward they pulled out the chair as well and they placed my brother on it. Mother had his blankets handed to her from the elevator, and she covered Ralfi. I took the chair and pushed to the other side of the corridor, where there were already many other beds, as I said before.

I pushed the chair close to the wall, on the side where windows opened onto the large lobby. I looked around. I saw about twenty-five beds lined up next to the wall. Some women were hugging each other and crying. Others, with the rosary in their hand, were praying. There were also some people who were not afraid, and were trying to comfort the others. Mother was also murmuring a prayer. Ralfi kept saying: "Calm! Calm!" but one could tell from his voice that he was more nervous than other people. In this way he was trying to calm himself. Every time a new explosion was heard, there were new tears and more fervent prayers.

I clutched at the windowsill overlooking the large hall and looked down. Some stretchers had been placed against the wall, and the nurses were ready to receive the wounded. Shortly afterwards the roar of a motor was heard, and a van entered the hall and stopped in the middle.

That van was not from the Red Cross, or from the firefighters, but simply from a private citizen, who, passing through the city just at the moment of the bombardment, picked up a few wounded from the street, put them on the van and took them to the Istituto Rizzoli which was the closest hospital. The most seriously wounded were taken to the operating room.

I remember as if l saw him in front of me today a man who got out of the van, sat on a stretcher, took off his hat and was running his fingers in his hair as if to comb it. That man had on his left shoulder a piece of shirt hanging, forming a round hole. But besides the shirt, a piece of skin was also missing. as well as a piece of flesh. I am not going to describe all the five hundred wounded who were taken to Istituto Rizzoli that day. There were women, children, old people. Many arrived already dead.

The vehicles of the firefighters entered the hall, unloaded the wounded and left again to go get others. Another firefighter vehicle arrived, the driver got off, and I saw him cry. Why is he crying, I wondered, maybe he has been wounded? A few minutes later I had the explanation of his sorrow: I saw another firefighter, covered with blood, being taken out of the cab of the vehicle. When the nurse put a hand on his heart and shook his head, I understood that he was dead. The driver was looking at his companion, who had died next to him while he was going through the city to rescue some wounded persons, and he was sobbing loudly. All the bystanders were moved. I was also moved, very moved.

It is heartrending to see a man, a soldier, cry. At that moment the horn of a car was heard. He then pulled himself together, got into his vehicle and drove it out to make room for another vehicle with its bleeding load. The body of the firefighter was taken to the morgue. I will not forget, for all of my life, those few minutes, that sobbing firefighter. I would like to praise the firefighters, but I cannot find the words. In fact, it is impossible to find them. If a soldier who kills many enemies is called a hero, how should we call one who saves those that someone else is trying to destroy?

The firefighter is the only soldier who saves instead of killing.

# VII.

My mother did not want me to see all these wounded people. Now however I realize it was a good thing that I looked.

When all the wounded had been taken, nobody was left in the large hall. There were only the bloodied stretchers pushed up against the wall. On the floor the blood stains were coagulating. I have just said it was a good thing that I looked. Yes, it was a good thing! I will never forget those wounded people, those arms, those legs, broken and bleeding, that flesh torn apart by the bombs. I will never forget that blood coagulating on the marble floor. That blood was a warning. That blood should have been seen by those responsible for the war, but not just by them. Above all it should have been seen by those who perhaps in the near future will want a war.

Then every time they were to look into a mirror they would see written on their forehead with that blood: "Murderer!" Every time they were to wash their hands they would feel that they are stained with the blood I saw flow from hundreds of wounds. And no soap can wash away that blood. If the ministers, the presidents, the kings, want to make war, why don't they kill each other? Who gives them the right to kill women, old people, children?

A doctor passed near us. His coat was red with blood. He was tired, his forehead was dripping sweat. "What a terrible day. Five hundred wounded came: the dead are twenty," he told us. "We have prepared five operating rooms, and we have operated without interruption until now."

An hour later the boy arrived who was going downtown with me when mother arrived. The young lady who had sent him to get the spool of cotton was anxiously waiting for him. Who knows what remorse she would have felt if something had happened to him. He rested a little because he was too upset to speak.

# POSTSCRIPT

*On the back of a photograph he sent to his father when he was 15 (in 1946) were written these words:* This is the face of a boy whose youth was taken from him, who doesn't know anymore how to cry or laugh, that life has crushed under the inhuman weight of cruel reality. In this photograph you see the mask of a face; if that mask were lifted you would see a mind troubled by life that too cruelly torments your son.

*Towards the middle of 1946, Anna decided to return to Merano to wait for further developments. Ralfi was sent to a sanatorium in Leysin. Leo entered middle school there and for the first time began to lead a more normal life.*

*In 1947, a plane ticket arrived from his father, and Leo became the first of his family to join Friedl in America.*

Questo è il volto di un giovane che non ebbe giovinezza, che non seppe né piangere né ridere, che la vita ha schiacciato sotto l'immane peso della cruda realtà. Su questa fotografia tu vedi la maschera di un volto; se la maschera cadrebbe, vedresti una mente turbata dalla vita, che tanto crudelmente si è accanita contro tuo figlio.

# AFTERWORD
## by Simi Berman and Nicholas Grosso

With all that Leo Berman was able to capture about those chaotic days, so much was never written down. Many details have been lost to time but a few stories have been kept alive through the stories he told his family, and are carried on now by all those who heard them and pass them on to others.

One particular story that Leo told over and over again was about a close call in Perugia. Following the bombing in Bologna when Leo, Ralfi, and Anna were at Istituto Rizzoli, Anna thought it was far too dangerous to remain there, and decided to go to Perugia, an old university town in Umbria, located on a hill halfway between Rome and Florence, where Rodrigo, a favorite old math teacher of her husband's lived. She thought he might be able to help, but when they arrived, they found him in a nursing home and in no position to offer any assistance.

All alone now in a strange town, she learned that the Catholic Church was helping Jews get false documents and find places for them to hide from the German army.

Fortunately, shelter was arranged for them by the Monsignor in one of the church buildings in the small village of Prepo on a nearby hilltop. To help conceal the fact that he was a Jew, Leo became an altar boy and did small chores for the parish priest, Don Guido Maccari, including helping to make sausages from a pig that had been slaughtered on the premises.

They stayed protected within the compound of the church through early 1945. But the fighting between the retreating Germans and the approaching Allies grew more intense as the Allied forces advanced northward. Leo could see and hear the shells exploding all around them. One shell came very close to hitting the church, making Anna again fear for their lives, and so she arranged to move the family from the church, an easy target at the center of the village, to a farmhouse a little more removed from the heat of battle.

The stone farmhouse to which they had fled was one of many properties belonging to a Signor Belluigi, who Leo, Ralfi, and Anna would soon find out was a fascist sympathetic to the Germans. One day, this man overheard Anna talking to Leo and his brother in German and immediately became suspicious, reporting them to the Kommandant in charge of the area. It didn't occur to him that she might be Jewish, he suspected her of being a spy, and the Germans acted upon this information at once. Taking her into custody, they interrogated her in the middle of an olive grove while the boys were hidden down the road.

The Kommandant had a large saber and the four soldiers with him rifles.

"We know that you are a spy, and that you understand German."

Anna pleaded, she was not a spy and did not understand German. She argued and cried, afraid her boys would be found and discovered that they were Jewish.

"Never mind, it is clear that you are a spy," the Kommandant ended any further appeal. "You are guilty and will be shot."

His men tied her to an olive tree.

"We offer you the choice of being blindfolded or not."

"I will not wear a blindfold, I will look you in the eyes until the last second of my life so that you may all feel guilty until the day you die."

The Kommandant lifted his saber and said to his soldiers, "When I bring down my saber, you shoot."

At that exact moment the thunder of bombs shook the ground and the Kommandant hesitated. In the next second, a German soldier came running over the hill shouting, "We must retreat! The Allied soldiers are here! They are only a mile away!"

"You stay here!" the Kommandant demanded. "We will be back for you."

It was a miraculous last-second rescue from death no one in the family ever forgot, not after Leo arrived in the United States in 1947, Anna in 1950, nor Ralfi the following year (after being delayed with tuberculosis of the bone).

In the United States, after so many close brushes with death, Anna kept her promise to God: to maintain the tenets of her faith, to keep a kosher home, and to strictly observe the sabbath and other religious holidays. And Ralfi went on to get married and have two children, settling in New Jersey.

Following his arrival in the US at age 16, Leo was sent to Cascadilla, a prep school for Cornell University in Ithaca, NY, where he studied civil engineering for two years. In 1951, he decided to leave Cornell to fulfill his Zionist dream of living in Israel, where he worked as a surveyor in the Negev. After 9 months there, he was drafted to fight in the Korean War but avoided active duty as a result of an infected ingrown toenail and a hernia operation. The ensuing years were captured in *The Brattleboro Reformer* profile. Following the war, "[he] decided to go back to Israel to live in a kibbutz. To that end, he studied architecture, became an electrician, and worked for a couple of years on a Zionist farm in New Jersey. In 1957, he returned to Israel with his bride, Simi. They worked there together for nearly a year [but then decided to return to America where Leo completed] his education in architecture at Columbia, [then he] opened his own firm in New York City. The firm's largest projects involved schools and research, sponsored by the city as part of the 1960s' movement of integration in urban schools." Berman committed the rest of his life to social justice. From free design projects for minority groups in New York City to community land trusts efforts in Vermont, he helped to construct and repair a world so devastated by hate and war.

I would like to bring Leo to life somehow but it is just too difficult to encapsulate a person in words. *The Brattleboro Reformer* profile mentions the mark he has left on downtown Brattleboro, "including the Granite building, the former Central Vermont Public Service substation on Arch Street, the Paramount and the Hooker Dunham building, where he [had] his office." But he has left just as great a mark on the lives of the people he came into contact with, the people he loved, and those who loved him. Among those he loved best were his son Mark and grandson Trevor; his role in their lives had a great impact.

# ABOUT THE AUTHOR

LEOPOLD BERMAN was born in Merano, Italy in 1931. He arrived in America in 1947 and shortly thereafter entered the Civil Engineering program at Cornell University in Ithaca, New York.

In 1951 he went to Israel where he worked as a surveyor in the Negev. He returned to the U.S. when he was drafted into the army in 1952. In 1956 he married and went back to Israel with his wife, Simi, to live on a kibbutz. In 1957 they returned to the States where he entered the 6-year program at the Columbia School of Architecture from which he graduated in 1963. After graduation the couple moved to Roosevelt, New Jersey where Leo lived and worked for six years

In 1969 they moved back to New York City where Leo started his own architectural firm, Berman, Roberts, Scofidio and Stromsten. Their projects included Educational Park in East New York, which involved working closely with the community to establish a hub school aimed at improving the educational facilities in that neighborhood, as well as the design and rehabilitation of Fort Greene Park in conjunction with A.E. Bye Jr., among others.

In 1981 the family moved to a farm in New Hampshire. There Leo opened his architectural office in Brattleboro, Vermont across the river, where he became engaged in many projects involving the preservation of old buildings. His work won the Vermont Award for Historic Preservation in 1992. In addition, his practice consisted of community oriented projects involving better housing for the indigent, mental health facilities, as well as houses and buildings for private individuals. Leo died in 2003.

# ABOUT THE TRANSLATOR

GIULIANA CARUGATI studied languages and literatures at the *Università Cattolica*, Milan, where she graduated *Summa cum Laude*, with a dissertation on American poetry. Her translations include a book (on economics!) from English to Italian, and from Renaissance-era Italian to English for an exhibition at the Jewish Museum on documents relating to Italian Jewry. Carugati has a PhD in Italian Literature, and has written two books about Dante Alighieri: *Dalla menzogna al silenzio* and *Il ragionare della carne*. She has taught at Emory University and the University of Michigan at Ann Arbor. Presently, she is writing a text mostly on Meister Eckhart.

# CROSSINGS
*An Intersection of Cultures*

*Crossings* is dedicated to the publication of Italian language literature and translations from Italian to English.

Rodolfo Di Biasio. *Wayfarers Four*. Translated by Justin Vitello. 1998. ISBN 1-88419-17-9. Vol 1.

Isabella Morra. *Canzoniere: A Bilingual Edition*. Translated by Irene Musillo Mitchell. 1998. ISBN 1-88419-18-6. Vol 2.

Nevio Spadone. *Lus*. Translated by Teresa Picarazzi. 1999. ISBN 1-88419-22-4. Vol 3.

Flavia Pankiewicz. *American Eclipses*. Translated by Peter Carravetta. Introduction by Joseph Tusiani. 1999. ISBN 1-88419-23-2. Vol 4.

Dacia Maraini. *Stowaway on Board*. Translated by Giovanna Bellesia and Victoria Offredi Poletto. 2000. ISBN 1-88419-24-0. Vol 5.

Walter Valeri, editor. *Franca Rame: Woman on Stage*. 2000. ISBN 1-88419-25-9. Vol 6.

Carmine Biagio Iannace. *The Discovery of America*. Translated by William Boelhower. 2000. ISBN 1-88419-26-7. Vol 7.

Romeo Musa da Calice. *Luna sul salice*. Translated by Adelia V. Williams. 2000. ISBN 1-88419-39-9. Vol 8.

Marco Paolini & Gabriele Vacis. *The Story of Vajont*. Translated by Thomas Simpson. 2000. ISBN 1-88419-41-0. Vol 9.

Silvio Ramat. *Sharing A Trip: Selected Poems*. Translated by Emanuel di Pasquale. 2001. ISBN 1-88419-43-7. Vol 10.

Raffaello Baldini. *Page Proof*. Edited by Daniele Benati. Translated by Adria Bernardi. 2001. ISBN 1-88419-47-X. Vol 11.

Maura Del Serra. *Infinite Present*. Translated by Emanuel di Pasquale and Michael Palma. 2002. ISBN 1-88419-52-6. Vol 12.

Dino Campana. *Canti Orfici*. Translated and Notes by Luigi Bonaffini. 2003. ISBN 1-88419-56-9. Vol 13.

Roberto Bertoldo. *The Calvary of the Cranes*. Translated by Emanuel di Pasquale. 2003. ISBN 1-88419-59-3. Vol 14.

Paolo Ruffilli. *Like It or Not*. Translated by Ruth Feldman and James Laughlin. 2007. ISBN 1-88419-75-5. Vol 15.

Giuseppe Bonaviri. *Saracen Tales*. Translated Barbara De Marco. 2006. ISBN 1-88419-76-3. Vol 16.

Leonilde Frieri Ruberto. *Such Is Life*. Translated Laura Ruberto. Introduction by Ilaria Serra. 2010. ISBN 978-1-59954-004-7. Vol 17.

Gina Lagorio. *Tosca the Cat Lady*. Translated by Martha King. 2009. ISBN 978-1-59954-002-3. Vol 18.

Marco Martinelli. *Rumore di acque*. Translated and edited by Thomas Simpson. 2014. ISBN 978-1-59954-066-5. Vol 19.

Emanuele Pettener. *A Season in Florida*. Translated by Thomas De Angelis. 2014. ISBN 978-1-59954-052-2. Vol 20.

Angelo Spina. *Il cucchiaio trafugato*. 2017. ISBN 978-1-59954-112-9. Vol 21.

Michela Zanarella. *Meditations in the Feminine*. Translated by Leanne Hoppe. 2017. ISBN 978-1-59954-110-5. Vol 22.

Francesco "Kento" Carlo. *Resistenza Rap*. Translated by Emma Gainsforth and Siân Gibby. 2017. ISBN 978-1-59954-112-9. Vol 23.

Kossi Komla-Ebri. *EMBAR-RACE-MENTS*. Translated by Marie Orton. 2019. ISBN 978-1-59954-124-2. Vol 24.

Angelo Spina. *Immagina la prossima mossa*. 2019. ISBN 978-1-59954-153-2. Vol 25.

Luigi Lo Cascio. *Othello*. Translated by Gloria Pastorino. 2020. ISBN 978-1-59954-158-7. Vol 26.

Sante Candeloro. *Puzzle*. Translated by Fred L. Gardaphe. 2020. ISBN 978-1-59954-165-5. Vol 27.

Amerigo Ruggiero. *Italians in America*. Translated by Mark Pietralunga. 2020. ISBN 978-1-59954-169-3. Vol 28.

Giuseppe Prezzolini. *The Transplants*. Translated by Fabio Girelli Carasi. 2021. ISBN 978-1-59954-137-2. Vol 29.

Silvana La Spina. *Penelope*. Translated by Anna Chiafele and Lisa Pike. 2021. ISBN 978-1-59954-172-3. Vol 30.

Marino Magliani. *A Window to Zeewijk*. Translated by Zachary Scalzo. 2021. ISBN 978-1-59954-178-5. Vol 31.

Alain Elkann. *Anita*. Translated by K.E. Bättig von Wittelsbach.
2021. ISBN 978-1-59954-170-9. Vol 32.

Luigi Fontanella. *The God of New York*. Translated by Siân E. Gibby.
2022. ISBN 978-1-59954-177-8. Vol 33.

Kossi Komla-Ebri. *Home*. Translated by Marie Orton.
2022. ISBN 978-1-59954-190-7. Vol 34.

www.ingramcontent.com/pod-product-compliance
Lightning Source LLC
Chambersburg PA
CBHW020212090426
42734CB00008B/1028